A TRUE BOOK™

Stop Bullying

LUCIA RAATMA

Children's Press®
An Imprint of Scholastic Inc.
New York   Toronto   London   Auckland   Sydney
Mexico City   New Delhi   Hong Kong
Danbury, Connecticut

Content Consultant

Dave Riley, PhD, is a professor in the Human Development & Family Studies Department at the University of Wisconsin–Madison. Colette Sisco is a faculty member in the Psychology Department at Madison College in Madison, Wisconsin.

Library of Congress Cataloging-in-Publication Data

Raatma, Lucia.
  Stop bullying/by Lucia Raatma.
    p. cm.—(A true book)
  Includes bibliographical references and index.
  ISBN 978-0-531-25521-6 (library binding) — ISBN 978-0-531-23921-6 (pbk.)
  1. Bullying—Juvenile literature. 2. Bullying—Prevention—Juvenile literature. 3. Aggressiveness in children—Juvenile literature. I. Title.
  BF637.B85R33 2013
  302.34'3—dc23   2012036006

All rights reserved. Published in 2013 by Children's Press, an imprint of Scholastic Inc.
Printed in China 62
SCHOLASTIC, CHILDREN'S PRESS, A TRUE BOOK™, and associated logos are trademarks and/or registered trademarks of Scholastic Inc.
10 11 12 R 22 21 20

Scholastic Inc., 557 Broadway, New York, NY 10012.

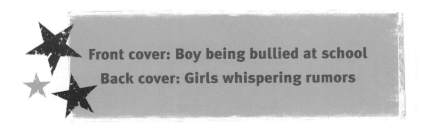

Front cover: Boy being bullied at school
Back cover: Girls whispering rumors

Find the Truth!

Everything you are about to read is true *except* for one of the sentences on this page.

Which one is **TRUE**?

T or F   Bullying only happens face-to-face.

T or F   One form of bullying is spreading gossip and rumors.

Find the answers in this book.

3

Contents

THE **BIG** TRUTH!

Many different kinds of people can act like bullies.

4 How to Prevent Bullying

Everyone is different in some way. ➡

Have you or someone you care about ever been involved in bullying?

CHAPTER 1

Understanding Bullying

Has someone ever teased you or one of your friends in a mean way? Have other kids **excluded** you from their group? Or have you ever excluded someone else? Bullying behavior includes making certain people feel different from others. It also includes making fun of other people and saying bad things about them. Bullies try to make their **victims** feel less powerful or less important. Bullying happens when these actions are repeated over and over.

About 90 percent of students have been bullied.

Bullying With Words

Many bullies call other kids names. They make fun of how kids look, commenting on their height or weight. They make fun of kids who have braces or glasses. They may target kids who need to use wheelchairs or other medical items. They tease kids about their family or where they live.

Bullies might exclude someone because he looks different or has different needs, such as a wheelchair.

Sometimes a person is bullied about her beliefs or background.

Some bullies focus on a person's race or religion. They may tease people about being from another **culture**. For instance, bullies may **taunt** someone for wearing religious clothing or jewelry. They may also bully people because of whom those people like or spend time with. Often bullies use their actions to try to prove that they are "better" than someone else.

Spreading rumors can hurt friendships.

A rumor could be an embarrassing secret, or it might not be true at all.

Spreading Rumors

Has someone ever said something about you that wasn't true? This probably made you angry. Or has someone you trusted told a secret you had shared? This probably upset you. Bullies use both secrets and things that aren't true to spread **rumors**. They talk about other people behind their backs and make those people feel embarrassed.

When people **gossip**, do you believe everything they say? Deep down, you may know that the stories could be made up. But sometimes people think gossip can be fun. Even people you thought were your friends can get caught up in spreading rumors. Have you ever done that to other people?

Gossiping can seem fun, but it is important to remember that it can also hurt people's feelings.

Bullying With Force

Sometimes bullying goes beyond words. Bullying can become physically harmful. Bullies may shove or push their victims. They may trip them or pull their hair. They may threaten them or their family members. Some bullies even hit or punch other kids. This can be scary for the people being bullied.

Some bullies steal or destroy items such as clothing, backpacks, or electronics.

Being bullied can make people feel unsafe and scared.

People who are bullied may worry that they'll be attacked on the playground or walking home from school. They may be afraid to ride the bus or go to school at all. Bullies use that fear to make themselves feel powerful. If bullies see a person as weak or scared, they may target that person even more.

Bullying might happen in the cafeteria, when someone is excluded from a table or conversation.

Excluding Others

Some bullies like to make sure their victims feel excluded from a group. They might say, "No, you can't sit here" or "You can't play our game with us." These kinds of actions make kids feel like a certain group doesn't accept them. They may feel that they aren't smart enough, pretty enough, or athletic enough.

Where Bullying Happens

Many bullies do their damage on playgrounds, at school, or in neighborhoods. Not all bullying happens face-to-face, though. Kids are also bullied on the Internet. Bullies use **social media** sites and cell phones to gossip about their victims. They write hurtful **posts** that many people can see. In this way, a mean rumor can spread in just seconds.

Being bullied can make life seem difficult and overwhelming.

CHAPTER 2

Knowing Who Is at Risk

If you have ever been bullied, you may wonder why you were targeted. You may think, "What did I do to deserve this?" Usually there is no good reason why bullying happens. Instead, bullies just like to feel powerful and important. They look for anyone who they believe is different in any way.

 Almost 50 percent of bullying victims tell their parents about being bullied.

Which Kids Are Bullied?

There is no solid explanation for why some kids are bullied and some aren't. But kids who are considered "different" or "not normal" are often targets. Maybe they are too tall or too short, too fat or too skinny. Maybe they wear glasses or use a hearing aid. Or maybe they're not good at sports. If you think about it, though, everyone is different in some way, right?

There is often no explanation for why a person is bullied.

18

Sometimes kids get lower grades on purpose to avoid being bullied.

Kids who are very smart are sometimes bullied, as are kids who struggle in school. Kids from different backgrounds may also be targeted. Bullies may decide to pick on kids because of the clothes they wear. Bullies sometimes focus on people who are different because the bullies don't understand them.

Some bullies are afraid of losing their status as part of the popular crowd.

Which Kids Are Bullies?

Some kids are more likely to bully than others are. Both boys and girls can be bullies. Some bullies are often very concerned with their popularity. They may want to show that they are "better" than everyone else. They may have friends who are bullies, too.

Bullies can also be outsiders. These are kids who are worried and **depressed**, and they may often feel unaccepted by their classmates. In fact, they may bully other people as a defense, to show that they are not as weak as they feel. These bullies often see violence as a good thing and have a hard time following rules. In many cases, bullies have parents who are not positively involved in their lives.

A bully might have difficulty at home with parents or a sibling.

Groups That Bully

Sometimes a group of kids may target a particular person to bully. They may see their victim as being different or weak. They may also pick on people who are not athletic or popular. They may target people who are poor or do not dress well. In some areas, gangs of kids bully each other, trying to prove who is tougher.

A group of kids might use their many members to intimidate or overpower one person.

More bullying takes place in middle school than in high school.

22

Kids sometimes think it is okay to bully others because their parents also bully people.

Throughout history, some groups have seen themselves as better than other groups. The groups may identify themselves by wealth or race or culture. Rather than accept the differences they see in others, they choose to pick on them. Often, these feelings are passed down from parents to children, and the pattern doesn't seem to end.

Signs of Bullying

Often, people who are being bullied are afraid to ask for help. They may hope the bullying will stop if they ignore it, but that is seldom the case. It is important that family and friends know the warning signs that someone is being bullied.

A person who is being bullied may sleep a lot and avoid going out. He or she may eat too much—or not much at all.

Someone who is being bullied may stop going to school or doing homework. His or her grades may drop.

A bullying victim may not be able to explain lost or damaged backpacks, clothing, electronics, or other items.

Someone who is being bullied may often feel sick or have injuries that aren't explained.

When someone is bullied, he or she may talk of **suicide** or having nothing to live for.

It can be scary to stand up to bullies, but it is important not to let bullying continue.

CHAPTER 3

How to Respond to Bullies

Bullying is not nice, and it is not fair. If you are the target of bullying, it is scary and depressing. You may want to hide at home or pretend everything is okay. If you see someone else being bullied, you may be afraid to speak up. But it is important to face what is going on. There are actions you can take to make things better.

Many kids who see bullying happen are afraid to speak up.

How to React

Being bullied can make you really angry. You may want to yell at the bully and say, "Stop!" But a strong reaction might be just what the bully is looking for. Instead, try just walking away with your head held high. If that doesn't seem possible, try just to stay calm, even when a bully is taunting you. Don't respond with challenges or insults of your own.

Try walking away if a bully is taunting you. Responding with your own taunts might only encourage the bully.

A few pushes
or a punch
can lead to a
serious fight.

If you ever see a bully starting a fight, don't stay and watch. Go and ask for help from a teacher or other school employee.

Try to avoid ever hitting a bully, even in self-defense. Often, hitting a bully will just lead to more problems. You might get in trouble as well. Make it clear that you don't care what the bully says or does. If a bully becomes physically violent or threatening, walk away and get help if you need to.

An adult can help you figure out what to do about bullying.

How to Get Help

If you're like most kids, you don't want to be a tattletale. However, there are times when you need an adult's help. If you or a friend is being bullied, find an adult you can trust. This might be your parent or another family member. You might also talk to your neighbor or teacher. Explain the problem and ask for advice. Often a teacher will know the bully well enough to understand what's going on.

Another way to get help is to talk to your friends. If some of your friends have joined in some of a bully's gossip, you may not know whom to trust. Think about one or two people you can count on. Explain how the bullying is affecting you, and ask for support. Just a few friendly faces each day can make all the difference.

Talking things over with one or two trusted friends can help you feel less alone and more confident.

When There Is Danger

Sometimes, bullying is not just about teasing and taunting. If you feel physically threatened, find ways to protect yourself. Don't walk home alone. Don't go into the school's bathroom alone. Instead, stay with a small group as much as you can. This will help you feel safer.

Timeline of Bullying

1999
Georgia becomes the first state to pass a law that discourages bullying and acts of violence among students.

2010
Phoebe Prince, a 15-year-old girl, commits suicide after being bullied in Massachusetts.

If the bully is making comments about hurting you or others, it is important to report it to someone. Some bullies are angry and want to hurt students, teachers, and other people. Talk to your parents or other trusted adults if the problem is serious. There are times when you have to get the school or the police involved in dealing with the bully.

2011
The White House holds its first Conference on Bullying Prevention.

2012
The movie *Bully* is released. It tells the story of several middle and high school students who are bullied.

Taking Control

You cannot control what a bully says or does, but you can take charge of your own life. If you're feeling scared, talk to your parents. Becoming involved in a new activity might help. Karate classes can help you work on your confidence and strength. Yoga can help you ease your fear and feel calmer.

Yoga and other physical activities can teach you ways to face your fear and your bully.

Having a hobby you love is a great way to combat bullying.

Writing things down can often help you think through a situation.

If you feel frustrated, write it down. Maybe you could write a letter telling the bully why he or she is being unfair. You don't need to send the letter. Just writing it can make you feel better. You can also write a list of all the things that are great about your life. This will help you focus less on the bully and more on the activities and people you enjoy.

Putting a stop to bullying is easiest to do as a team.

CHAPTER 4

How to Prevent Bullying

One of the best ways to prevent bullying is to talk about it. Just bringing attention to it can help make dealing with the problem easier. Talk about bullying with friends you can trust. Discuss how it affects you and other people you know. You can also talk with adults and your friends about ways to put a stop to it.

When you support a friend who has been bullied, you send the bully a message.

Finding Solutions

Bullying often happens in places where there are no adults. These places could be bathrooms or certain parts of the playground. They could also be on school buses because the driver can only focus on the road. Figure out how to make those places safer. Ask adults to be more aware of the problem. Encourage kids to stick together.

Other kids can help stop a bully, especially when adults are not around.

Boys are more likely to use physical violence in bullying.

It's a lot less scary to stand up to a bully as a group.

Often, there really is safety in numbers. If everyone in your class agrees to stand up to the bully, then the bully will feel outnumbered. He or she will probably back down. In fact, the bully may even feel embarrassed. As a group, make it clear that bullying behavior is not okay.

Have you ever bullied someone?

Are You a Bully?

Think about your own behavior. Do you tease other kids? Do you call people names? Do you shove or hit people when you're angry? Do you make fun of people because of what they wear? If you sometimes do these things, try to understand why. Maybe you're having trouble at home. Maybe you're feeling frustrated. Or maybe you have been bullied.

If you are bullying others, many kids may not want to be around you. You might feel powerful for a moment, but it will probably not last long. Other kids will notice your behavior and reject you. To have good, real friends, you need to learn how to be nice to other kids. Try surprising people by being nice to someone for no particular reason. How do the people around you react?

Girls and boys have about the same likelihood of being bullied.

You don't need a reason to be nice to someone or lend a helping hand.

The Bully Effect

Research shows that people who are bullied are more likely to suffer from depression. They are also more likely to have poor grades and drop out of school. If the bullying is extreme, they may even commit suicide.

People who bully others are more likely to get into fights. As they get older, they are more likely to commit crimes and be physically violent. They may also be more likely to abuse alcohol and drugs.

Showing respect is the easiest way to make friends you can count on.

Show Respect and Stop Bullying!

Remember, everyone deserves **respect**. You should respect your friends and classmates, and they should respect you. If people are being bullied, they are not being respected. Take time to talk about respect with friends and trusted adults. Treat people the way you want to be treated. Find ways to appreciate other kids and enjoy everyone's differences. ★

True Statistics

Number of bullies in U.S. schools: 2.1 million

Number of students who miss school each day because they are afraid of bullies: 160,000

Percentage of fourth- through eighth-graders who have been bullied: 90

Number of students in kindergarten through 12th grade who were either a bully or a victim of bullying in 2010: 1 in 7

Percentage of students who have seen bullying take place at school: More than 50

Percentage of students who have told an adult when they are victims of bullying: 42

Number of students who drop out of school or change schools because of bullying: Nearly 1 in 10

Percentage of students who see bullying as an ongoing problem: More than 70

Number of states that have passed bullying-prevention laws: 49

Did you find the truth?

F Bullying only happens face-to-face.

T One form of bullying is spreading gossip and rumors.

Resources

Books

Blume, Judy. *Blubber*. New York: Dell Yearling, 2004.

Ludwig, Trudy. *Confessions of a Former Bully*. Berkeley, CA: Tricycle Press, 2010.

Murphy, Alexa Gordon. *Dealing With Bullying*. New York: Chelsea House, 2009.

Shapiro, Ouisie. *Bullying and Me: Schoolyard Stories*. Chicago: Albert Whitman & Company, 2010.

Visit this Scholastic Web site for more information on bullying:
★ www.factsfornow.scholastic.com
Enter the keywords **Stop Bullying**

Important Words

culture (KUHL-chur) — a group of people with similar ideas, customs, traditions, and way of life

depressed (di-PREST) — sad and unhappy with life

excluded (ik-SKLOOD-id) — kept from joining or taking part in something

gossip (GOSS-ip) — to talk about other people's personal business

posts (POHSTS) — messages, videos, photos, or other information on a Web site

respect (ri-SPEKT) — a feeling of admiration or high regard for someone or something

rumors (ROO-murz) — stories or reports that are spread by word of mouth but may not be true

social media (SOH-shuhl MEE-dee-uh) — Web sites that help people connect with each other

suicide (SOO-i-side) — the act of killing oneself on purpose

taunt (TAWNT) — to try to make someone angry or upset by saying unkind things about him or her

victims (VIK-tuhmz) — people who are hurt, killed, or made to suffer

Index

Page numbers in **bold** indicate illustrations.

About the Author

Lucia Raatma is a writer and editor who enjoys working on books for young readers. She earned a bachelor's degree in English from the University of South Carolina and a master's degree in cinema studies from New York University. She likes writing about all sorts of subjects, including history, conservation, wildlife, character education, and social media. She lives with her husband and their two children in the Tampa Bay area of Florida.